The Great
Aztecs

by L. L. Owens

Perfection Learning®

About the Author

Lisa L. Owens grew up in the Midwest. She has been writing since she was a young girl, and she has always enjoyed learning about how people lived in earlier times.

She currently works as a writer and editor in Seattle, where she lives with her husband, Timothy Johnson.

Other books by Ms. Owens include *Looking Back at Ancient Greece, Inside Ancient Rome, The Mysterious Ancient Maya,* and *Eye on Ancient Egypt.*

Credits

Cover Design: Emily Greazel
Book Design: Deborah Lea Bell

Image Credits: ©*Gianni Dagli Ortis/CORBIS* cover; Bodleian Library, University of Oxford MS. Arch. Selden. A. 1, fol. 2r p. 7; CORBIS Traditional pp. 28, 39 (bottom), North Wind Picture Archives p. 14 (top)

ArtToday(some images copyright www.arttoday.com) pp. 1, 3, 4, 8, 9, 10, 11, 12, 13, 14 (bottom), 15 (bottom), 16, 17, 18, 19, 20, 22, 23, 24, 25, 26, 27, 29, 30, 31, 32 (bottom), 33, 34, 39 (top), 40 (top), 42 (bottom), 43, 45 (top), 46, 48, 50, 51, 52; Corel pp. 5, 21, 32 (top), 35, 36, 40 (bottom), 42 (top), 44, 45 (bottom), 47; Dover pp. 6, 15 (top), 37, 38, 53, 56

For information, contact
Perfection Learning® Corporation,
1000 North Second Avenue,
P.O. Box 500, Logan, Iowa 51546-0500.
Tel: 1-800-831-4190 • Fax: 1-800-543-2745
perfectionlearning.com

Paperback ISBN 0-7891-5742-x
Cover Craft® ISBN 0-7569-0910-4
2 3 4 5 6 7 PP 09 08 07 06 05 04

Contents

Timeline 1100–1522 A.D.

1100   The Aztecs leave Aztlán. They begin a long search for a new home.

1195   The Aztecs arrive in the Valley of Mexico.

1250   The Aztecs settle near Lake Texcoco.

1325   The Aztecs build Tenochtitlán, their capital city. They begin conquering neighboring lands.

1375   Acamapichtli becomes the first Aztec ruler.

1428   The Aztecs form the Triple Alliance with Texcoco and Tlacopan. They seize the valley. This is the beginning of the Aztec Empire.

1440   Montezuma I begins his 28-year rule of Tenochtitlán.

The ruins of Temple Mayor in modern-day Mexico City, which was founded on the site of Tenochtitlán

1452   Tenochtitlán is destroyed by flood. **Famine** spreads from 1452 to 1454.

1487   The Great Temple at Tenochtitlán is dedicated. About 20,000 prisoners are **sacrificed**. The Aztecs move south into Mayan territories.

1502   Montezuma II becomes ruler. The Aztec Empire is at its height.

1519   Spanish **conquistador** Hernán Cortés arrives in Mexico.

1520   Montezuma II is killed in a riot by Aztecs who don't trust him.

1521   Spanish troops conquer Tenochtitlán.

1522   Tenochtitlán is rebuilt as Mexico City. It becomes the capital of the Spanish colony of New Spain.

Introduction
Who Were the Aztecs?

The Aztecs were **nomads**. They moved from place to place. They were searching for a new homeland. Each time they tried to settle down, other tribes drove them away.

The Aztecs finally settled in Mexico during the 14th century. They had been traveling for 200 years!

Much of the information about this time in Aztec history comes from **legends**.

The Aztecs did as they were told. According to a legend, they found the special eagle on an island.

The island was in the center of Lake Texcoco in the Valley of Mexico. No one lived there. So the Aztecs quickly claimed the land.

Here the Aztecs built the city of Tenochtitlán. This was the center of what was to become the powerful Aztec Empire.

The year was 1325.

Soon the Aztecs built temples, houses, and other structures.

The Legend of Tenochtitlán

The Aztecs searched for a home. They had the help of Huitzilopochtli. He was the god of sun and war.

This god led them to a swampy island. He told the people to look for an eagle.

Huitzilopochtli said, "The eagle must be sitting on a cactus that grows from a rock. The eagle must have a snake in its mouth. When you find such a sight, you have found your home."

This artwork shows how the Aztecs founded Tenochtitlán.

Symbols in the Story

The eagle in the story **symbolizes** the sun. Aztecs believed the sun gave them life.

The cactus represents the human heart. They believed that the sun god needed hearts to live.

Take a look at the modern Mexican flag. It features an eagle sitting on a cactus! It also has a snake in its mouth.

From 1345 to 1440, the entire Valley of Mexico was in turmoil. States struggled for power. Each kingdom wanted to rule the valley.

The early Aztec civilization existed a long time ago. All dates in this book are based on **scholars'** best guesses.

8

The years 1440 to 1521 saw Aztec expansion and conquest. The Aztecs fought everyone in their path. They were a fierce and powerful people.

At its peak, the Aztec Empire was home to up to six million people.

In 1521, the great Aztec Empire fell at the hands of Hernán Cortés. This happened during the Spanish Conquest.

The Spanish destroyed most Aztec objects, artworks, buildings, and records. That has made it hard for us. We are eager to learn about Aztec history.

Aztec **ruins** are still studied today. They can be found in modern-day Mexico City and surrounding areas.

Read on for more about how the great Aztecs lived!

Hernán Cortés

Chapter 1

Aztec Life

What was Aztec life like? The people went to school. They enjoyed flowers, music, dance, art, and poetry. They worked. They followed a religion. They had laws and leaders. They fought wars. They threw parties.

We still study this old **civilization**. Maybe it's because Aztec life was so different from modern life.

Or maybe we study it because we have so many things in common. Those things can make our differences seem even more amazing.

The City

About 200,000 people lived in Tenochtitlán. People often traveled in canoes through canals connecting the different districts. There were four city districts.

- Flowery Place

- Mosquito **Fen**

- Herons' Home

- Place of the Gods

Many roads joined parts of the city. Along the way, homes, palaces, ballcourts, schools, government buildings, and temples in the shape of **pyramids** could be found.

Model of Tenochtitlán

The Class System

There were three main **classes** in Aztec society.

- **Nobility:** This class was made up of rulers, chiefs, and nobles. Rulers controlled empires and major cities. The chiefs controlled smaller areas. They held high military positions. Noblemen held important government, military, and religious positions.

- **Middle Class: Merchants** and **artisans** were considered middle class. Merchants traded luxury goods and served as spies. Artisans made fine crafts. They sculpted and worked with gold, feathers, and **mosaic**.

Aztec artisans

- **Commoner Class:** Commoners included farmers, fishermen, and craftspeople.

Women weaving

The Roles of Women and Men

Women worked hard. They raised the children. They prepared food and kept their homes in order. They trained their daughters to cook, spin, and weave. And they advised their husbands.

Women made clothing, rugs, and blankets for their families. They also made the rulers' clothing. That was one way that workers paid taxes.

A few women were allowed to serve as priestesses. Farmers' wives traded in the flower and fruit markets.

Men worked hard too. They provided for their families. They kept their homes in good repair. And they trained their sons to fight.

Warrior in jaguar fur

Aztec Jobs

- builders
- fishermen
- stonecutters
- sculptors
- doctors
- warriors
- farmers
- priests
- merchants
- porters
- **scribes**
- judges

Fishermen

Rulers

The ruler, or *tlatoani*, was very wealthy. He lived in a great palace in Tenochtitlán. He was the head of the government, army, court system, and the priesthood.

People called the ruler the Great Speaker. He was considered the most important person in society. There were 11 known Aztec rulers. In most cases, each was related to the previous ruler.

Would You Believe . . . ?

A ruler's deputy was the *ciuacoatl*. The word meant "snake woman." Yet a man always held this post!

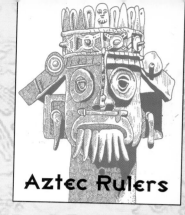

Aztec Rulers

- **Acamapichtli**
  1367–1387
- **Huitzilhuitl**
  1391–1415
- **Chimalpopoca**
  1415–1426
- **Itzcoatl**
  1427–1440
- **Montezuma I**
  1440–1468
- **Axayacatl**
  1469–1481
- **Tizoc**
  1481–1486
- **Ahuitzotl**
  1486–1502
- **Montezuma II**
  1502–1520
- **Cuitlahuac**
  1520
- **Guatemotzin**
  1521–1524

15

Priests and Priestesses

Priests and priestesses were powerful and respected. They had many roles.

- They made sacrifices to the gods.

- They warded off evil spirits.

- They were religious leaders.

- They were teachers.

- They studied the stars.

- They helped solve problems.

About 5,000 priests lived in the Great Temple of Huitzilopochtli. They were serious about their duty to their god.

To set themselves apart, priests grew long hair. They did not wash. They painted their skin black. And they wore black cloaks.

Warriors

Military training for boys began while they were still in school. Skilled warriors were valued. They were needed to help protect the empire.

Warriors hoped to join either the Eagle or Jaguar society. Membership meant that they had proven themselves mighty and brave.

Merchants

Aztec merchants were wealthy. They were known as *pochtecas*. They traded their goods in the local market and with other cities.

Aztec Trading Goods

- cotton
- **cacao** beans
- flowers
- rugs
- feathers
- slaves
- spices
- jewelry
- herbal medicines
- **incense**
- household goods
- stones

Merchants' travels could be dangerous. They had to protect their goods from thieves.

Rulers had their merchants spy on foreigners. Most merchants spoke many languages.

Yacatecuhtli was a god of the merchants. His name meant "Lord Nose."

Doctors

Doctors understood much about the human body. They had cures for all sorts of things. They used many **herbal** medicines.

Injury or Illness	Doctor's Remedy
Broken leg	Tie splints to the leg.
Deep cuts	Sprinkle **obsidian** powder on the wound.
Earache	Pour liquid rubber in the ear.
Chest pains	Give an herbal **tonic**.
Cold	Place a drop of dew into each nostril twice a day.
Fever	Have patient take a steam bath to release evil spirits.

An Aztec Doctor's Advice for Pregnant Women

- Pray to one of the goddesses of women every day.
- Do not look at the sun. Your baby will be deformed if you do.
- Do not chew gum. It will cause your baby's mouth to swell to twice its normal size.
- Do not look at ghosts. If you do, you could harm your baby.
- Carry wood ash with you to ward off ghosts after dark.

Porters

A porter's life was hard. Porters carried goods on their backs. They traveled between cities, from the country to the city. A porter often walked up to 25 miles a day.

A strap held a porter's load on his back. The strap looped around his forehead.

The load could be anything from food to building materials. Sometimes porter groups even carried noblemen.

Slaves

Slaves worked for the nobility. They worked farmland, helped construct buildings, and acted as servants.

Some slaves were prisoners of war. Some were criminals who had been sentenced to slavery. For these people, slavery lasted a lifetime.

Some slaves were children of parents who had sold them for the money. Others

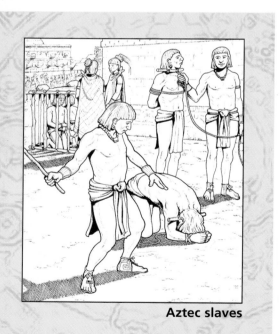

Aztec slaves

had lost bets or were paying off debts. These people were allowed to buy their freedom once they saved enough money.

Aztec Rules
for Leading a Model Life

- Do not sleep too much. If you do, you will become a sleeper and a dreamer.

- Be careful in your travels. Go peacefully and quietly. Do not **throw your feet** or go jumping. If you do, you will be called a fool and shameless.

- Speak very slowly. Do not speak fast, and do not pant or squeak. If you do, you will be called a groaner.

- Do not stare into another person's face.

- Do not **eavesdrop** and do not **gossip**.

- When you are called, do not be called twice. If you are, you will be thought lazy or **rebellious**.

- Do not dress **vainly** or decorate yourself fantastically. Dress carefully so you do not trip over your cape. But do not shorten your cape or expose your shoulders.

- Above all, eat and drink in **moderation**.

2

Chapter

What Did the Kids Do?

Home Life

Children were raised to be honest, responsible, and skilled. They were also taught to expect hardship.

They had many chores. They studied with their parents. They played games. They learned music. And, like all kids, they were punished when they misbehaved.

Today, the punishments those children received seem cruel. One punishment was to tie up the children. Then they were left outside in the cold.

Parents also might hold children's faces close to a smoking pile of chili peppers. As the children breathed, the pepper's oil would burn their nostrils, throats, and lungs.

Schooling

Noble children attended schools called *calmecacs*. The schools were next to the temples.

Girls and boys went to separate calmecacs. Priests were their teachers. The children studied **astronomy**, warfare, history, poetry, religion, and government.

Commoners' children—boys only—attended their own school, or *telpochcalli.*

Aztec Studies

- flowers
- citizenship
- religion
- art
- music
- counting
- warfare
- history
- science
- writing
- dance

Female children of commoners stayed home. They studied with their mothers. The goal was to train them for marriage. Girls learned spinning at age 4 and cooking at age 12.

Cooking

Chapter

3

The Basics: Food and Clothing

What Aztecs Ate

Maize is a type of corn. It was the main food source of the Aztecs. They used it to make tortillas, tamales, and **porridge**, or *atole*.

They ate many fruits, vegetables, and water creatures. They loved to add spices to their dishes.

On special occasions, they ate deer, turkeys, and the meat of hairless dogs. They also made a chocolate drink from cacao beans.

Maize

Most Common Aztec Foods

- tomatoes
- mushrooms
- beans
- shrimp
- water-fly larvae
- grubs
- gophers
- snails

- avocados
- peppers
- fish
- insect eggs
- tadpoles
- rabbits
- frogs

Most Aztecs ate twice a day. They rose at dawn but did not eat breakfast. Their first meal of the day was their main one. They ate it several hours after rising. Then they took naps, or *siestas*.

They ate a second meal at midday. Most working people went to bed at sundown.

Rich merchants and the nobility stayed up late. They gave parties and ate a third meal.

Nobles could afford to have chocolate every day. They also ate expensive foods.

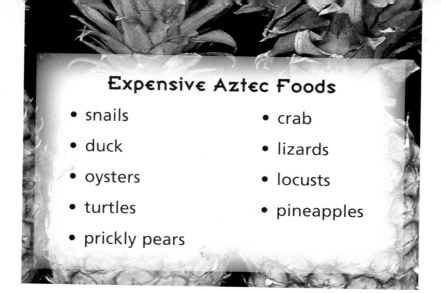

Expensive Aztec Foods

- snails
- duck
- oysters
- turtles
- prickly pears
- crab
- lizards
- locusts
- pineapples

Montezuma II

Montezuma II's servants prepared 300 different dishes for a single meal—just for him. He was a very fussy eater. He ordered that many dishes to be sure something would interest him.

Smart Farming

The Aztecs needed to grow food to survive. But there was no natural farmland in Tenochtitlán. Much of the city was built on wetlands. So farmers decided to create the necessary environment.

How Did They Do It?

First the Aztecs made giant mats. They wove them from reeds. They placed the mats on top of the water.

Next they made a fence out of branches

and twigs. They secured the mats with rocks tied to the sides. Then the mats were sunk into the water.

Then the Aztecs piled mud, manure, and rotting vegetables on the mats. This was their version of **compost**. The Aztecs continued this until the pile was above the water's surface.

This whole structure was a *chinampas*.

The next step was to plant willow trees. The farmers surrounded each chinampas with new plantings.

Why plant the trees? Well, willow trees grew fast. Their roots formed large balls in the soil. These kept the dirt from washing away into the lake.

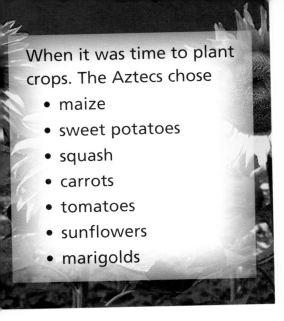

When it was time to plant crops. The Aztecs chose

- maize
- sweet potatoes
- squash
- carrots
- tomatoes
- sunflowers
- marigolds

The Aztecs successfully created "farmland" in the middle of a lake. And the lake provided their crops with a constant source of water.

What the Aztecs Wore

Commoners' clothing was quite plain. Women wore skirts that wrapped around the hips and waist. Men wore loincloths and sleeveless cloaks.

Each man carried a small pouch. He'd wear it slung over his shoulder under his cloak. The pouch held **coca** leaves and **amulets**. He chewed on the leaves during the day. The amulets brought him good luck.

The nobles dressed in colorful, woven cotton clothing. They also had bright, feathered headdresses.

Chapter 4

Religion

Beliefs and Ceremonies

Religion was a big part of Aztec life. The people worshiped many gods and held many beliefs, which helped guide their lives.

Statue of Quetzalcóatl

Aztec Beliefs

- Gold, silver, and jade had magic powers.
- The sun fought darkness every night. It rose every morning to save humankind. It would lose its daily battle without blood from humans.
- The earth was flat.
- There were 13 heavens and 9 hells.
- After death, people lived on in the afterlife.

The Aztecs built lavish temples and pyramids to praise their gods. They also honored them with stories and drawings.

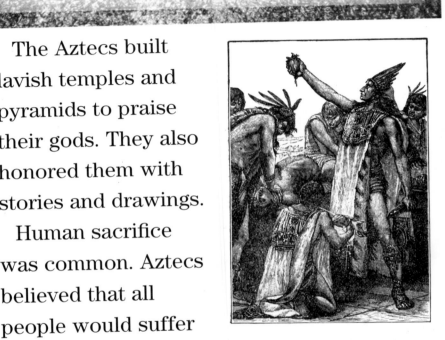

Human sacrifice was common. Aztecs believed that all people would suffer unless a few were sacrificed.

But they sacrificed many more than just "a few." The Aztecs believed that the sun god needed human blood every day. So they had to kill people *every day.*

Each year, about 10,000 to 15,000 people were sacrificed to the gods.

The largest Aztec sacrifice ever was huge. It's almost unbelievable. Scholars found evidence that up to 80,000 people were sacrificed during one bloody four-day festival of the gods!

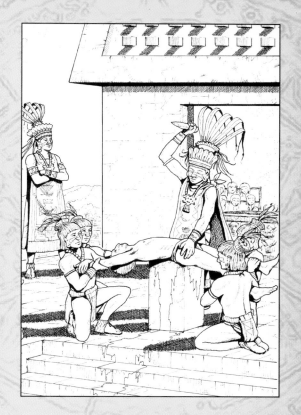

How Were Sacrifices Chosen?

Some—but not many—volunteered for sacrifice. They believed in dying to help their people. They also believed that they would have a happy afterlife.

In other cases, priests chose people. Families offered their sick. Warriors captured men. Criminals were sentenced and sacrificed. Rulers offered their slaves.

How Were Sacrifices Made?

Here's what might have happened on Gods' Feast Day.

Priests dressed as the gods. They took a captive to the top of an extinct volcano.

The priests watched the evening star. They waited for it to reach the top of the sky.

The high priest cut into the captive's chest. Then he lit a fire on the captive's heart. He ripped the heart right out of the man's body!

The high priest lifted the heart to the heavens. He offered it to the sun. Then he placed the heart in a sacred dish.

With the ceremony over, the captive's body served no purpose. The priests rolled it off its perch. It fell into the mouth of the volcano. And it landed on the pile of bodies sacrificed before it.

How the
Sun and Moon Came to Be

Legend says that the gods tired of living in darkness. They decided to bring light to the world.

All the gods met at the home of the gods and goddesses. They needed to decide which god would become the sun. At first, nobody wanted to be the sun. They knew it meant being sacrificed.

Finally, two gods came forward. One was Tecuciztecatl, a proud and wealthy god. The other was Nanauatzin, a sickly and poor god.

At midnight, the two gods approached the raging fire. It was time for the sacrifice.

Tecuciztecatl threw himself into the flames. But the flames rejected him.

He tried four times. Four times, the flames threw him out.

Nanauatzin decided to try. He ran straight into the middle of the roaring fire.

As he entered, he waved to Tecuciztecatl. He called out, "Follow me!" And he disappeared.

Tecuciztecatl rushed at the spot that had swallowed Nanauatzin. He disappeared too.

The next morning, Nanauatzin rose in the east—as the sun! He filled the sky with his blinding red light. He was so bright that no one could look directly at his face.

Later, Tecuciztecatl showed up. He was following in the sun's path. He shone brightly too.

The gods decided that they did not want two such bright lights.

Quetzalcóatl fixed things. He picked up a rabbit. And he threw it at Tecuciztecatl's face.

Tecuciztecatl was wounded. His face was permanently darkened. From then on, he became known as the moon.

The sun and the moon have had a place in the heavens ever since.

Aztec Gods and Goddesses

The Aztecs believed in about 1,000 gods! Here are just a few of them.

- **Chalchiuhtlícue:** Goddess of lakes and streams.

- **Chantico:** Goddess of the **hearth**.

- **Chicomecoatl:** Goddess of maize.

- **Coatlícue:** Goddess of pain and poverty. She wears a necklace made of a heart and claws. Her skirt is made of snakes.

- **Huehuetecti:** God of fire.

- **Huitzilopochtli:** God of war, sun, and the nation. He holds a shield and a fire-breathing snake.

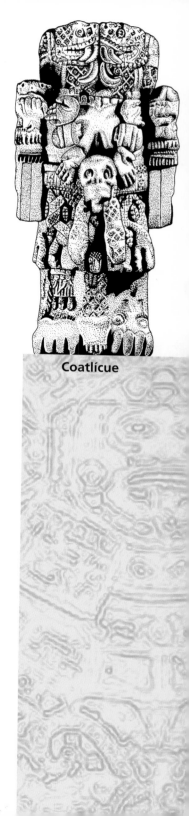

Coatlícue

37

- **Mictlantecuhtl:** God of the dead. Aztecs believed that people who died of natural causes lived with this god. As they traveled to their new home, a wind of knives sliced off their skin. They spent their afterlife as skeletons.

Quetzalcóatl

- **Quetzalcóatl:** God of creation, self-sacrifice, wind, knowledge, arts and crafts, and the priesthood. He took the form of a feathered snake.

- **Tezcatlipoca:** God of creation, fate, magic, war, and death. He's called "Smoking Mirror" and represents the dark side of life. He has a missing foot. He dragged the earth out of the waters before the gods created man. The earth monster tried to stop him and ate his foot.

Xipe Totec

- **Tlaloc:** God of rain. He was half human and half alligator. He has fangs and eye rings.

- **Tlazolteotl:** Goddess of childbirth.

- **Tloque Nahuaque:** Lord of Everywhere. This is the Aztecs' supreme force, both male and female.

- **Xipe Totec:** God of spring, new life, and suffering. He wears a human skin.

- **Xochipilli:** Prince of flowers. Also the god of dawn, dance, and love. He stands for **eternity**.

Xochipilli

5

The Sun-Stone Calendar

The Aztecs studied the passage of time. They knew it was important to understand it. Their calendar was the Sun Stone. The sun god was pictured in the center.

The Aztecs used the Sun Stone to follow two calendar systems. One was the "counting of the days." The other was the "counting of the years."

Would You Believe . . . ?

The Sun Stone itself was carved in the mid-15th century. It weighs more than 25 tons!

Counting of the Days

This was the religious calendar. The Aztecs borrowed it from the ancient Maya.

The calendar was divided into 20 periods. Each period had 13 days, or *trecenas*.

Each period had a name. And each day had a number. Aztecs believed that a different god watched over each day. Depending on the god, some days were good. And some days were bad.

If a baby was born on a "bad" god's day, the parents waited to name the child. They believed that naming a child on a "good" day canceled out the bad god's spirit.

Counting of the Years

This calendar measured time. It followed a 365-day solar cycle. The Aztecs used it to plan crops and to predict **solar** eclipses.

The cycle was divided into 18 periods. Each period had 20 days, or *veintenas*.

Who Were The Ancient Maya?

The Maya lived in the Mexican areas of Yucatán, Chiapas, and Tabasco. They also lived in Guatemala, Honduras, and what is now Belize.

Like the Aztecs, the Maya were victims of the Spanish Conquest.

Five days were left over. These "days of nothing" were treated as the bridge between the old year and the new year. People believed these days brought bad luck.

The Two Calendars Meet

The "counting of the days" and the "counting of the years" calendars moved together. They were both shown on the Sun Stone.

Once every 52 years, the same day in each calendar fell at the same time. That 52-year Aztec cycle is like our 100-year cycle, or *century*.

Chapter 6

Criminal Justice—
The Aztec Way

When someone committed a crime, or was accused of one, he or she went to court. Citizens served on the jury. They listened to both sides of the story.

Judges decided whether the accused was innocent or guilty. When found guilty, Aztecs suffered harsh penalties.

It looks like it was a good idea to stay out of trouble!

Crime	Punishment
selling poor-quality goods	property taken away
becoming drunk	head shaved and house destroyed for first offense; death for second offense
wearing cotton clothes (if a commoner)	death
cutting down a live tree	death
moving a field boundary	death
handling stolen property	sold into slavery
stealing small goods	sold into slavery
stealing expensive goods, stealing often	death
kidnapping	sold into slavery
committing treason	death, property taken away, land destroyed, and children sold into slavery

Chapter 7

Art, Music, Dance, and Games

Art

Artisans included scribes, metalworkers, stonecutters, potters, and feather workers.

Items Artisans Made

- **pictograms**
- statues
- knives
- fishhooks
- headdresses
- jewelry
- ornaments
- needles
- shields
- fans

Would You Believe . . . ?

Montezuma II had a grand headdress. It was made from the feathers of more than 250 tropical birds. Feathers were plucked from parrots, macaws, and quetzals.

Aztec Instruments

- trumpets
- rattles
- whistles
- copper bells
- temple drums
- panpipes
- shells
- flutes

Scribes made paint out of **minerals**, vegetables, insects, and shells. Other artists' materials included jade, obsidian, crystals, bone, rock, clay, wood, and feathers.

Music and Dance

The Aztecs loved music and dance. Both played big parts in religious ceremonies.

Children learned to dance and sing at age 12. They also learned to play instruments.

The Aztecs told stories through dance. They used dance to share news, tell history, and please the gods.

Games

Patolli was a favorite board game. Adults played it with jade pebbles and dry beans. Players bet their pebbles against the number of beans they thought they could win.

Tlachtli was a popular ballgame played on an I-shaped court. There were two teams. Each had a rubber ball. The object was to shoot the balls into a high hoop. The team who made the first basket won.

Would You Believe . . . ?

It was against tlachtli rules to shoot the ball with your hands. You had to shoot it with your knees.

Not surprisingly, the game often took several hours!

Chapter 8

Language and Writing

Nahuatl

Nahuatl was the Aztecs' language. Several words we use today come from Nahuatl.

Nahuatl word	English word
áhuacatl	avocado
chílli	chili
choclátl	chocolate
tamalli	tamale
tomatl	tomato

Have you wondered how to pronounce the Aztec city of Tenochtitlán? Try tay–noch–TEET–lon.

Here's a long Nahuatl word to think about.

notlazohtiachcauhtzitzihuane

It means, "Oh, my beloved elder brothers." Can you figure out a way to say that word?

The Aztecs loved poetry. Below is an ancient Nahuatl poem. The poet's name was Nezahualcoyotl. That's pronounced ness–ah–wall–COH–yohtl.

Like gold that I cast,
Like jade that I pierce,
Like beads that I string,
That is my song.

Here's a fragment of another Nahuatl poem. It's by an unknown poet.

Can it be lived on earth?
Not for always on earth: just a little here.
Even though it be jade, it breaks,
Even though it be gold, it breaks,
Even though it be quetzal feathering, it rips,
Not for always on earth: just a little here.

Picture Writing

Scribes and priests used picture writing to tell stories and record history. They had hundreds of symbols.

Nouns were easy because a picture stood for each word. So a picture of a pepper stood for the word *pepper*.

Words other than nouns were hard to draw. They usually just gave a clue to the meaning.

A whole sentence was made up of several symbols drawn in a row.

Books

An Aztec book was called a *codex*. The plural form is *codices*.

Codices were made of fig-bark paper and folded like an accordion. Covers were made of wood.

You could read a codex from left to right or top to bottom.

Chapter 9

The Spanish Conquest

The Spanish invaded the Yucatán **Peninsula** in 1519. Hernán Cortés and 500 conquistadores had one goal—conquer the Americas.

They started with Mexico's great Aztec Empire.

Montezuma II ordered his men to greet the Spaniards with food and gold. Cortés and his men set up camp.

On November 8, 1519, Cortés waged war against the Aztecs. He seized Montezuma II and his palace. Cortés wanted control of Tenochtitlán.

Montezuma II wanted his people to make peace with the Spanish. The people did not agree. They started a riot.

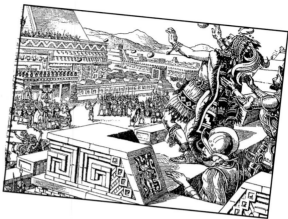

Soon Montezuma II was dead. His own people had stoned him to death.

The fighting continued. Many lives on both sides were lost.

The Spanish defeated the Aztecs on August 31, 1521. They crushed Tenochtitlán.

The Spanish tore down houses, burned crops, and destroyed temples and all Aztec records. Then they built Mexico City on top of the ruins.

Cortés and his men had shattered one of the greatest empires in history.

Now, nearly five centuries later, a new generation of Aztecs has a vivid history to share.

Glossary

amulet	lucky charm
artisan	person who creates fine art
astronomy	study of the solar system
cacao	dried seeds of a South American evergreen used for making cocoa and chocolate
civilization	group of people who live in a social group
class	group that shares the same social status
coca	South American shrub
compost	rotting vegetation used to make soil richer
conquistador	Spanish soldier in the conquest of the Americas in the 16th century A.D.
eavesdrop	to listen secretly to what others are saying privately
eternity	all time; forever
famine	period of great food shortage

fen	low land that is entirely or partially covered with water
gossip	to spread rumors
hearth	home
herbal	made from plants
incense	material that produces a fragrance when burned
legend	story handed down from generation to generation
merchant	one who sells goods
mineral	something not animal or plant, such as rock, sand, coal, and so on
moderation	within reason; not to excess
mosaic	small tiles used to make artistic patterns
nobility	group of people given higher status than others
nomad	person with no permanent place to live
obsidian	hard, dark natural glass formed from lava

peninsula	portion of land sticking out into the water
pictogram	ancient or historical drawing
porridge	cooked cereal such as oatmeal
pyramid	structure with a base and four triangular walls that meet at the top
rebellious	disobedient
ruins	remains of something destroyed
sacrifice	to offer as a gift
scholar	one who has knowledge
scribe	writer or recorder of events
slave	someone owned by and forced to work for another person
solar	relating to the sun
symbolize	to represent; to stand for
throw your feet	kick or skip; have too much spirit or fun
tonic	liquid medicine
vainly	showing too much pride in one's appearance

Index

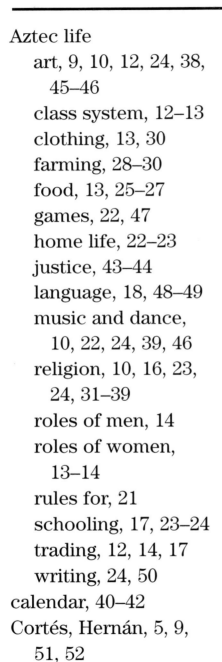